JOHN HARBISON

T0087801

THE VIOLIST'S NOTEBOOK

BOOKS I AND II

Commissioned by Joan and Roderick Nordell
for Emmanuel Music.
First performance October 12, 2003
at Emmanuel Church, Boston, Massachusetts

AMP 8225
First Printing: November 2006

ISBN 978-1-4234-1740-8

Associated Music Publishers, Inc.

DISTRIBUTED BY
HAL•LEONARD®
CORPORATION
7777 W. BLUEMOUND RD. P.O. BOX 13819 MILWAUKEE, WI 53213

The Violist's Notebook, Books I and II

The name Bartolomeo Campanioli is lost in the mists of history. I confess that I know nothing about him except that he wrote viola etudes—inventive, musical, satisfying viola etudes. In general no pedagogical etudes need have any place in the education of a musician (I remember especially the miserable pedantry of the famous Kreutzer violin studies). But Campanioli is recalled by a few violists as a good composer (probably a violist himself), a congenial spirit, a musician who encouraged us to expand our technique by dangling an elegantly musical carrot on a stick.

As I began keeping my violist's notebooks I thought of Campanioli, his practical, subversively challenging communications with his violist colleagues. Book I was accumulated, in the margins of larger pieces, over three years. Book II was composed in six days, one a day, as a self-imposed project, at Bogliasco, near Genoa.

These etudes are more compositional than technical studies. Each is dedicated to a violist, mostly hard-core but a few doublers are included. The pieces can be performed in any sequence or grouping.

—John Harbison
January 2003

durations:

Book I, ca. 10 minutes
Book II, ca. 10 minutes

Commissioned by Joan and Roderick Nordell

THE VIOLIST'S NOTEBOOK
Book One

John Harbison

I.
(Marcus Thompson)

II.
(Betty Hauck)

Larghetto, preciso

♩. = 63

III.
(James Dunham)

IV.
(Kim Kashkashian)

Appassionato ♩. = 60–69

V.
(Mary Ruth Ray)

Rubato, improvisando

VI.
(Marcus Thompson)

Book Two

I.
(Sally Chisholm)

Moderato cantabile ♩. = 72

8

II.
(Randy Kelly)

Giocoso, deliberato

♩ = 56–69

f non legato

dim.

p

cresc.

mf

f

(10)

11

ff

dim.

rit.

14

p ——————————————— *pp*

più legato

III.
(Lenny Matczynski)

Lamentoso ♩ = 66

10

IV.
(Shem Guibbory)

V.
(Jaime Laredo)

12

VI.
(Lynn Ramsey)